Backpacking for Beginners

The Essential Traveler's Guide to Backpacking and Hiking Around The World

ISBN-13: 978-1518852701

ISBN-10: 151885270X

Contents

Introduction

I want to thank you and congratulate you for downloading the book *Backpacking for Beginners: The Essential Traveler's Guide to Backpacking and Hiking Around The World.*

This book contains proven steps and strategies on how to approach your first backpacking adventure. It provides tips from the people who know best: backpackers themselves.

Many backpacking guide books are filled with so much information that you may feel overwhelmed and confused. This book, however, cuts to the chase and gives you the information you really need. At the end of each chapter there are useful links to websites where you can find out more about specific aspects of backpacking.

Chapter 1: Ready, set ...

So you've decided to take some time off to go exploring. With so much world to see out there, the hardest part of your journey will be deciding where to go. The next step will be to find a way of getting there.

Choosing your destination

With so many different options when it comes to destinations for backpackers, you may want to start by reading up about different places. Start with easy-to-read travel articles of the 'Twenty destinations you have to visit before you die' variety to get an idea of what there is to see and experience. As you read about different places, make a list of the ones that really appeal to you. Maybe there is a certain attraction you've always wanted to see, or maybe you would like to go somewhere with great beaches or a vibrant nightlife, or maybe you want to hike the Appalachian Trail or the Camino de Santiago.

Once you have your travel wish list, it's time to look at the details. How much time can you afford to be away? How much money do you have to finance your trip? What will the weather be like at the destination at the time you're planning on going?

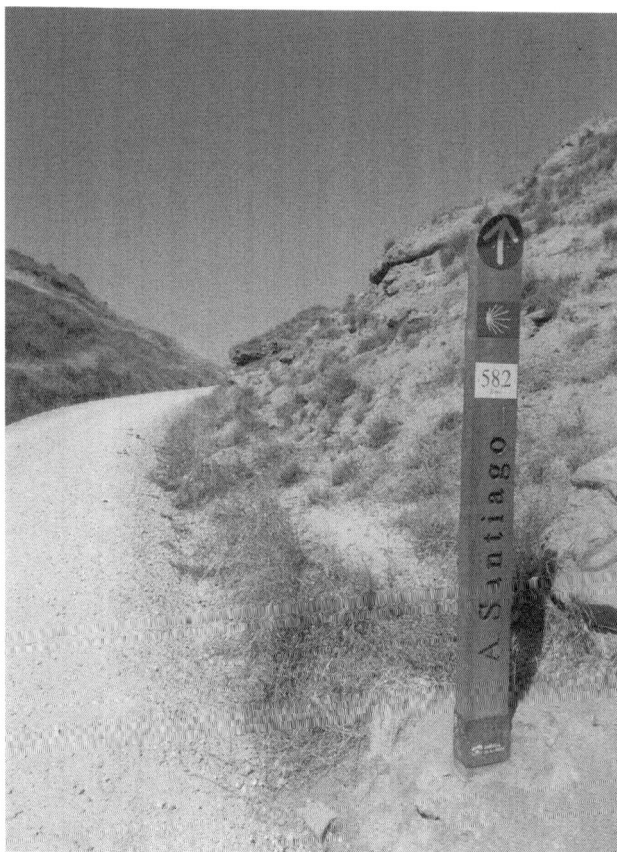

One of the great things about taking a few months for a backpacking trip is that it allows you to see and experience several things in a region. For example, do you want to see ancient ruins, learn about fascinating indigenous cultures, hike through the jungle, try some adventure sports and fit in some surfing or diving? Then Central America may be the region for you.

For your first backpacking adventure, it's best to visit a region that has an established backpacking trail. In this way you can experience the exotic while still being able to enjoy the familiar. You'll meet lots of people with similar interests. You can also pick up tips from the more seasoned travelers and the expats who quite never managed to leave once they found paradise. Some of the most popular areas for backpackers are Mexico, Central and South America, South East Asia and Europe.

Flights

Once you know where you want to go, you need to figure out how to get there. Your flight will probably be your greatest expense, so you need to do some research to find the best option. There are plenty of websites that find and compare flights for you: You simply need to google 'cheap flights' and type in your destination. If this is too daunting a task, ask your local travel agent to help you.

There are different types of flight that you may consider:

- A straight-forward return ticket: With a return ticket, you fly back from the same airport that you flew into. This is a good option if you're going to travel in a relatively small region where a circular route makes sense, such as South East Asia, India or Southern Africa.

- An open-jaw ticket: With this type of ticket, you fly into one city but your return flight is from a different city entirely. For example, you may fly into London, explore Europe and fly back home from Athens. This is a great option for larger regions or regions that are geographically more linear, like Central America, so that you don't have to retrace your route for your flight home.

- A round-the-world (RTW) ticket: This type of ticket is perfect for you if you're planning an epic adventure that will span several continents. Airline alliances often offer RTW tickets that include several stops. For example, you may set out from Los Angeles, fly to New York, then to Buenos Aires, from there to Johannesburg, on to Kuala Lumpur and then back to Los Angeles. You can buy a ticket that's valid for as long as a year, so that you can take your time exploring each region.

- An air pass: An air pass works on the same principle as an RTW ticket but is restricted to a region, such as Latin America, Europe or Africa.

To find the best flight deals, be flexible. Sometimes you can find a much cheaper flight simply by moving forward your date of departure by one or two days.

Visa and entry requirements

An important aspect to consider is the visa and entry requirements for people from your country. Even if you don't need to pre-apply for a visa to enter a certain country, you may be required to pay an entrance fee that can be as much as $100, so you'll have to know what to budget for. You can find the necessary information through your country's foreign-affairs department. Check the information regularly, since regulations change from time to time.

Useful links

For ideas about destinations and other handy backpacking advice:

www.backpacking-spirit.com

For great advice about choosing flights:

www.independenttraveler.com/travel-tips/air-travel

For information about visa and entry requirements:

www.visahq.com

For information about visa and entry requirements for US passport holders:

http://travel.state.gov/content/visas/english/general/americans-traveling-abroad.html

For information about visa and entry requirements for UK passport holders:

http://visacentral.co.uk/visa-quick-check.php

For information about visa and entry requirements for Australian passport holders:

http://visalink.com.au/visa-quick-check.php

Chapter 2: Money matters

One of the reasons why backpacking is so popular, especially with students and young adults, is that this way you don't need a fortune to go traveling. However, you still need to save up and budget for your trip.

How much money do you need?

Your budget really depends on your destination. There are countries in Asia, Latin America and Africa where you can get by with as little as $20 a day, while in the developed world, you'd need at least $50 a day. This budget would include accommodation in hostel dorms, eating street food or in basic restaurants and using public transport rather than taxis.

Before your trip, research average costs of living at your destination. The website www.budgetyourtip.com is a good place to start. It gives you the average travel costs for different countries on the backpacking trail, as well as the costs for popular destinations within these countries. Most guide books also give you a ballpark daily budget as well as average costs in different hostels and restaurants.

Another option is to use an online travel budget calculator to get an idea of how much money you'll need. Try several different ones to get a more accurate figure.

Once you've budgeted for the bare daily minimum, add as much money as you can for emergencies or for those times when you'd like to splash out on a private room, an adventure sport, a meal in a nice restaurant or any other little luxury.

Tips for saving money

As you travel, you'll quickly pick up tricks and tips that will save you money. Here are some of them:

- Stay in a hostel with a kitchen. Then buy groceries from the local market and cook your own meals.

- Discover the joys of street food and budget restaurants serving set meals. This is a great way to try the local cuisine too!

- Refill your water bottle. At many hostels, you can do this free of charge.

- Choose a hostel that offers free Wi-Fi or internet access.

- Don't assume that a dorm bed is the cheapest option. Sometimes it works out cheaper to share a private room with one or two other people. You may even get a private bathroom!

- Do your own laundry.

- Use local transport instead of tourist shuttles.

- Walk whenever you can and save transport costs.

- If it's available at your destination, buy a travel pass. These usually work out cheaper per trip.

- Buy beer from the store and hang out at the hostel instead of at a bar.

Cash or card?

Traveling with wads of cash on you is not a good idea. If you get robbed, you'll lose everything. Besides, it's easier to overspend when you have more cash in hand.

However, remember that hostels and budget hotels don't always accept credit cards.

Moreover, especially in more remote areas there aren't always ATMs available. Therefore, try to have enough cash for a couple of days and keep it well hidden in your luggage. You may want to keep some emergency US dollar as well, since this is one of the easiest currencies to exchange. When you go out, take only what you'll need and keep the rest locked in the hostel's safe or the locker provided.

These days most backpackers use their debit cards instead of traveler's checks. Before your trip, check with your bank that your card will work in other countries and make sure you have the bank's international number for lost or stolen cards. It's a good idea to have two cards: one MasterCard and one Visa card. This is because ATMs often take only one type of card and if there's only one ATM at your destination, you'll be stuck if you have the wrong card. A credit card is useful for emergencies.

Working, studying and volunteering

It's not unusual for a backpacker to run out of money during the trip. If this happens to you or you simply want to replenish your funds, you may have to find some work along the way. This isn't always the easiest thing to do, but being able to speak the local language or having special skills will help you. The possibilities for the type of work you may want to do are endless: from bartending at your hostel's bar to teaching English. Another option is to find some kind of job that you can do over the internet, such as writing or designing websites. This way you won't have to worry about those pesky work permits.

A great way to justify your trip to your parents or your employer is to take some time to study something. It can be a two-week course at a language school, a one-day cooking course, a PADI diving course: Again, the possibilities are endless. Many of these courses are quite cheap and they'll truly enrich your experience.

Volunteering is becoming an increasingly popular option for travelers too. Many NGOs rely on volunteers for doing their work. You can find projects online or ask around at your destination. Just remember to research the project and organization beforehand, since some aren't as noble as they'd like you to think and may actually do more damage than good.

Useful links

Travel cost calculators: There are several handy ones, including those at www.trekhard.com, www.euro-backpacker.com and www.solotravel.org.

Useful tips for carrying money: http://www.lonelyplanet.com/travel-tips-and-articles/76996

Information about work and volunteer opportunities: http://www.workingabroad.com/

Chapter 3: What to pack

When it comes to deciding what to take on your trip, the most important rule is to pack light. Lugging around a heavy, bulky backpack is not only exhausting but it makes catching crowded public transport a nightmare.

For wilderness hikes, the rule of thumb is generally that your backpack shouldn't weigh more than about 30% of your body weight. This of course includes your tent, food, sleeping bag and cooking utensils. If you're going on a trip where you'll be using public transport a lot, your main concern should be the airline's weight restrictions for luggage, which is generally in the region of 20 or 25 kg.

Gear

For the duration of your trip, your backpack will contain your life. It's one of the most important investments you'll make, so don't buy the cheapest one at Walmart. Instead, go to a specialist outdoor and camping store where a knowledgeable assistant can help you make your choice.

Generally a 60-liter pack is perfectly fine: not too big and not too small. Backpacks are like shoes, though: Try on a few different ones to see how they fit your body. Your backpack shouldn't cause strain on your back, shoulders or waist.

Backpacks basically come in two categories: top-loading and front-loading. Top-loading packs are narrower and more comfortable to carry, so they're best for long-distance hikes. A front-loader is great for traveling, though, since it opens up just like a suitcase. It's easy to pack and to find your stuff without having to dig too much. You can also secure the zippers with a padlock. However, most front-loaders don't offer much back support, so you won't want one of these if you're going on a long trek through the wilderness.

These days you can also choose backpacks with wheels. These are useful if you're going to travel in cities with smooth road or sidewalk surfaces. However, in much of the developing world, you'll be walking on cobbled streets, dirt roads and other uneven surfaces where the wheels will be useless and will only add to the weight of your pack.

A tent and sleeping bag are only really necessary for wilderness adventures. For the typical gap-year trip, you'll be staying in hostels where bedding is provided. If you want, you can take a sleeping sack, which is basically like a sleeping bag made of sheets. This comes in handy in hostels where the bedding isn't the cleanest. A cheap alternative for a sleeping sack is a duvet cover.

You may also want to take a smaller day pack for carrying your money, sunscreen, water and other day-trip essentials.

Clothes

The clothes you'll need depend on your destination and personal preferences. The following is a basic list for travel in warmer climates. If you're going to travel in cold climates, you'd need a thicker jacket, thermal underwear and extra warm clothes.

• Two pairs of strong but lightweight long pants, or a pair of pants and a long, wide skirt: Cargo pants are versatile and if style isn't important, you may want to consider pants that can be converted into shorts. Don't be tempted to take jeans, though: They're heavy and they take forever to dry. Besides, in warm climates they will be too hot and can cause painful chafing. You may want to substitute one pair of pants for sweatpants or leggings that you can use as sleepwear too.

- Two T-shirts that are made of a quick-drying fabric: You can always pick up more T-shirts during your trip.

- A long-sleeved shirt or T-shirt: These come in handy for keeping away mosquitoes, protecting your skin from the sun, keeping out the chill and getting you into religious buildings where modesty is required.

- A pair of longish shorts if you want: Short shorts are a no-no, especially for women, since local populations often prefer modest clothing. In some places you may get away with longer shorts but a skirt is generally a better choice. Men may prefer boardshorts that can double as swimwear.

- Swimwear: For women, a two-piece is generally fine but don't take the tiniest bikini you can find. Modesty should be your watchword.

- A sarong: You can pick up a sarong at most beach destinations. It's one of the most versatile pieces you can have in your backpack: You can use it for covering up quickly, as a towel or beach towel or even as a nice skirt for a night out. Guys can wear sarongs too and will find them a godsend on lazy days or when they suffer from chafing.

- Underwear: How many pairs you take is really up to you, but three is a good number. This way, you can wear one pair and have an extra dry pair while you wash the third pair. Women may want to include a good sports bra. While it's easy enough to buy underwear on the road, remember that it's often difficult to find larger sizes.

- Socks: Like underwear, how many pairs of socks to take is a personal choice. If you're going to travel in hot climates, you won't need more than three pairs unless you're going to do some serious hiking.

- A rain poncho: There are many types of rain gear that you can pack but a poncho is the most versatile. You can use it to cover your backpack at the same time, for instance. If you go for the type of poncho that fastens at the sides, you can even fold it open and let it double as a ground cover.

- A belt: A belt isn't strictly necessary, but on longer trips you'll probably lose weight and will need something to keep your pants from falling down as you jump off buses. Besides, a belt can come in handy in many other ways too.

Shoes

You're going to do a lot of walking, so your shoes should fit comfortably, be strong and be 'broken in' rather than brand new.

Hiking boots are heavy and bulky, so only take them if you're going to do some trekking. For shorter day hikes, a pair of good trainers is normally sufficient.

In warmer climates, you'll want a pair of sandals. Sports sandals with adjustable straps and made of synthetic material are great, since they're comfortable and dry quickly. Make sure your sandals have a heel strap. You don't want to lose your shoes as you get onto or off public transport!

A pair of flip-flops is great for the beach, for the shower or on days when you want to rest your feet. However, you can buy these locally, often for as little as $2.

Toiletries

Since basic toiletries are readily available in most places, you only need to take a few items. It's even better when you take them in travel sizes and if you can take multi-purpose items, such as a three-in-one shampoo, conditioner and shower gel. What you take is up to you but along with toothpaste and toothbrush, shower gel, shampoo, razors and deodorant, these items will come in handy:

- Sunscreen: There is nothing worse than the straps of your backpack rubbing against sunburned shoulders, so take sunscreen – and wear it!

- Insect repellent: Especially in more tropical climates, you'll need some way to keep away mosquitoes, sandflies, ticks and other bugs.

- Nail clippers: It's an item that many people forget. However, nail clippers are useful not only for keeping your nails short but can also double up as scissors to cut through string or thread.

- Lip and skin balm: Even in humid climates, your lips and skin can become dry and chapped. A multi-purpose balm can be used on lips, elbows, heels and any other dry bits.

- Dental floss: Even if you don't floss regularly, dental floss is a great item to slip into your backpack. You can use it for many non-dental purposes, from making it double up as strong thread to using it as an emergency clothesline.

- Condoms: These generally aren't too hard to find at your destination but it's always a good idea to have some ready. Just because you're far from home doesn't mean you don't have to practice safe sex!

- Sanitary products: Sanitary pads and tampons aren't too difficult to find but can be quite expensive. It may be hard to find your preferred type too. You may want to consider taking a menstrual cup instead, since it's reusable, more environmentally friendly and takes up less space than other sanitary products.

- Medication: If you use prescription medication, be sure to take enough for the duration of your trip. You may be able to find generic substitutes at your destination but these may be more expensive. Some painkillers and anti-diarrhea meds are good to have in your luggage too.

- First-aid kit: Many backpacking guides will tell you to take a first-aid kit with an array of bandages, syringes and other items. Unless you're going to the middle of nowhere, you won't need all these items. However, take at least a small tube of antiseptic cream and some adhesive plasters for blisters and other minor injuries.

- Diaper cream or calamine lotion: In hot and humid climates, there is a real risk of chafing, especially if you're a bit overweight. This can be painful and very uncomfortable. Two miracle products to treat chafed skin overnight are a zinc oxide-based diaper cream or calamine lotion. The diaper cream can double as an emergency sunscreen while the calamine lotion will also soothe rashes, insect bites and even sunburn.

Other useful items

The following items are not essential but will come in handy:

- A laptop, netbook, tablet or smartphone: Since the majority of hostels offer Wi-Fi, being able to connect to the internet will help you keep in touch with those at home. You can also use them to research your next destination, book transport and accommodation or simply to pass the time. Some backpackers even use their gadgets for working as they travel. However, don't become so dependent on your gadgets that you stop interacting with other travelers or seeing the places you've come to see.

- An alarm clock: At times you'll have to catch an early bus or shuttle and will need to wake up at the crack of dawn.

- Earplugs: You'll be eternally grateful for your earplugs when you're staying somewhere with noisy neighbors or construction going on right outside your room.

- A flashlight: When you have to get up really early, a flashlight will help you find your stuff without having to switch on the light and disturbing the other people in the dorm. Many developing countries struggle with intermittent power supply too, so a flashlight will come in handy during power outages. If you're going on a hike in the wilderness, of course, a flashlight will be your only source of light.

- A laundry bag: A simple cloth bag is great for putting your laundry in, especially if you're not going to wash your own clothes. However, a pillowcase can do the same job just fine.

- A guide book: Many people rely only on the internet for information on destinations but a guide book has the advantage that you can consult it anytime, anywhere, without having to worry about battery power. The maps are usually much easier to read than Google Maps too.

- A phrase book in the local language: In some areas you'll be hard-pressed to find someone who can speak English. A phrase book will make communication infinitely easier.

- A multitool or Swiss Army knife: Since airlines won't allow you to have sharp objects in your carry-on bag, only take a multitool or knife if you're okay with your backpack being checked luggage.

- A set of plug adapters

- Extra batteries and an extra memory card for your camera

- A basic sewing kit: Some needles and thread are very handy for repairs to torn clothes or buttons that come loose. Add a thick, strong needle too for repairs to shoes and backpacks.

- A combination lock: Not all hostels are equal when it comes to security. When the lock on your door doesn't work, when the locker

31

doesn't come with its own lock or when you simply want to lock the zippers on your backpack together, a combination lock is best. This way, you don't have to worry about carrying a key.

• A hammock: There's nothing like swinging in a hammock on the beach on a lazy day. Especially in Latin America, hostels may even have spaces where you can string your hammock and save on accommodation costs.

• Photocopies of your passport and other travel documents: You may also want to scan in all your documentation and let someone at home keep copies that they can email to you in an emergency.

Useful links

Links to reviews of backpacks:
http://studenttravel.about.com/od/campinggear/a/backpackreviews.htm

A comprehensive list of what to pack, with advice for different climates:
http://www.travelindependent.info/whattopack.htm

A useful list of the types of plug and wall socket used in different regions:
http://www.worldstandards.eu/electricity/plugs-and-sockets/

Chapter 4: Accommodation and transport

During your trip, you'll be faced with a huge variety or accommodation and transport options. These tips will help you make a more informed decision:

Accommodation

The type of accommodation you choose really depends on your budget and how much you're willing to spend.

- Campsites: Camping tends to be your cheapest option but not all countries have good camping facilities. However, some hostels will allow you to camp in their garden for a small fee. Just remember that going the camping route means you'll have to carry your own tent, bedding and cooking gear.

- Backpacker's hostels: When choosing a hostel, think about your own needs. If you want a good night's sleep, for example, a party hostel will be a terrible choice unless you have a set of earplugs. You're completely within your rights to ask to see the rooms before making your decision. Also compare room rates, since a private room shared with fellow travelers may work out cheaper per person than a dorm bed.

- Small budget hotels and guesthouses: These are often a great alternative to backpacker's hostels. You may even find a private room with your own bathroom and cable TV for less than a dorm bed in a popular hostel.

Your guide book is a great place to start when looking for accommodation. You'll also find options on travel sites such as TripAdvisor. Through word-of-mouth you may find hidden jewels, so also ask the people you meet along the way.

Many first-time backpackers struggle with the question of whether or not to book their accommodation ahead. You don't really need to, unless you're visiting a destination during peak tourist season or around special events such as religious festivals. However, it's a good idea to book accommodation for your first night or two before you catch your flight. This way you won't have to wander around looking for a place to sleep after being in a cramped plane for several hours. Especially if you need to take a long flight to get to your destination, you may also prefer a private room for those first few nights, so you can rest.

Transport

As a backpacker you'll often have to make the choice between taking public transport and taking a tourist shuttle. Tourist shuttles are common in popular backpacking towns and are a convenient way to get from one destination to the next. Some may even pick you up or drop you off at your accommodation, so they're excellent for long trips or when you don't feel confident enough yet to ask for directions.

The main drawbacks of tourist shuttles are that they're more expensive and a little, well, sterile. If you really want to experience the local culture and meet not only the locals but maybe their chickens too, consider taking public transport such as second-class buses or boats. The journey may take longer and may be back-breaking but it will definitely be more memorable. Public transport is generally not as unsafe as some people will have you believe.

Useful links

For accommodation, reviews and online booking almost anywhere in the world: www.hostelworld.com

Chapter 5: How not to be *that* tourist

Traveling can bring out the worst in some people. You'll see them during your journey: the tourists who show no regard for local customs, engage in illegal or exploitative activities, haggle over three cents or just generally offend wherever they go. Through their behavior they not only make themselves look bad but they also spoil everyone else's day and can even taint their nation's image overseas. Besides, some tourist behavior can have a very negative impact on the local community.

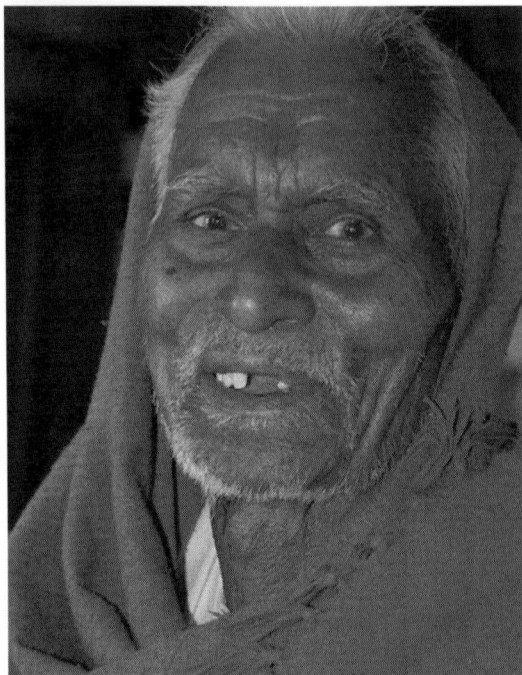

In order not to be one of *those* tourists, the keyword to remember is 'respect': respect for the locals, for your fellow travelers, for the environment and for yourself. Here are some tips:

• Show some consideration for your fellow travelers. For example, late at night when others are trying to sleep, keep it down.

- Treat the local population with respect. They are not your servants and just because they may not speak English very well or at all doesn't mean that they're inferior to you. In fact, they will really appreciate it and may even be more helpful if you make the effort to learn some of their language, even if it's just the basic greetings and the words for 'please' and 'thank you'.

- Dress modestly. Even in beach towns, you shouldn't walk around shirtless or only in your bathing suit unless you're actually on the beach. See how the locals dress and use that as a yardstick for how much flesh you can show.

- When you enter a religious site, cover your head, take off your shoes or follow whatever other custom is expected.

- Don't expect everyone to do everything your way. People in other countries have their own way of doing things and it's been working just fine for them for years.

Environmental responsibility

Tourism can have a devastating impact on the environment. If you go on a nature excursion, do so with a tour operator who has a reputation for being environmentally responsible. You don't have to disturb and scare animals in their natural habitat just so you can get a better picture. Also, take your litter with you until you can throw it in a bin. Even if the local people litter, it doesn't mean you have to join them.

In national parks, wildlife reserves and other protected areas, follow the rules. There's a good reason why park officials may ask you not to feed the animals, not to stray off the marked trails or not to make fires. You don't want your illegal campfire to be the cause of an inferno that destroys thousands of acres of pristine forest.

It's important too to find out what the local environmental issues are so that you don't inadvertently cause more damage. So, do some research. That cute little lion cub you're cuddling may be bred for canned hunting, for instance, while making that coral trinket has probably caused irreparable damage to a fragile marine ecosystem.

Social responsibility

You only have to visit a soulless, inauthentic tourist town to see the negative social impact of tourism on a community. Again, find out what the issues are and also remember these tips:

- Don't buy, sell or use drugs. Ever. In the first place, it's illegal in most countries and can carry severe penalties, even the death penalty. In the second place, where drugs are readily available and seem to be tolerated, there is a very dark side that you don't always get to see. With drug trafficking come higher crime rates and violence, gang activity and police corruption, not to mention the destruction of families.

- Think very carefully before you give to beggars, especially kids, or you may perpetuate a culture in which tourists are seen as walking cash machines. If someone really seems down and out, rather buy them a meal or give them something warm to wear. It's better to give your money to an NGO that can help people in need.

- Don't bribe police officers or border officials. Bribing will only perpetuate corruption.

- Know when and how to haggle. In some cultures haggling is almost expected in markets but in a more formal shop the prices are usually fixed. First compare prices to get an idea of the average price of an item. If a vendor seems to want far more than the average, you may indicate in a friendly way that it's a little steep for you. The vendor can then decide whether or not to start bargaining. When you do haggle, remember that it's not a competition where you simply have to get the goods for the lowest price possible. Vendors also have to make a living, so play fair.

- Use local services, stay in locally owned hostels, eat in locally owned restaurants and buy locally produced goods as often as possible. This way your tourism dollars will actually help the people whose home you've come to visit.

Useful links

For tips and responsible tour ideas:
www.responsibletravel.com

For more about the issues and some travel tips:
www.sustainabletourism.net or
www.ethicaltraveler.org

For more about the issues as well as ethical tour operators and volunteer organizations:
www.tourismconcern.org.uk

Chapter 6: Staying healthy and safe

While most people manage to complete their trip without any major problems, it's always a good idea to be prepared for possible mishaps. If you take responsibility for your health and safety into your own hands, you will be more aware of the hazards and will do more to avoid problems.

First up, get the most comprehensive travel insurance you can afford. In this way, if something goes wrong, you won't have the added stress of not having enough money for medical help or for replacing stolen goods. In fact, having travel insurance means that if you do need a doctor, you can afford a private one who speaks English. Remember though to check the fine print on your insurance policy, since many policies won't cover injuries sustained during extreme or adventure sports.

Staying healthy

About one or two months before you leave, visit your doctor or local travel clinic to find out which vaccinations you'll need. Some countries will require you to have certain vaccinations, such as for yellow fever, before they'll allow you entry. Among the vaccinations commonly recommended for travelers are those for hepatitis A, hepatitis B, rabies and tetanus.

Like death and taxes, it's a certainty that at some point during your journey, you'll suffer from a bout of traveler's diarrhea. It's normally caused by bacteria that you may have picked up through contaminated food or water or eating with utensils that weren't as clean as you'd thought. It's also more common in developing countries and you can contract it anywhere, from street food to a meal in a high-end restaurant. Practicing good hygiene and avoiding food that is obviously dodgy will reduce the risk, though.

Normally you don't have to worry too much: It will pass in a day or two, so simply take it easy

47

and stay hydrated. You may want to take some rehydration salts or sports drinks to help with the hydration bit. If you also have a fever or very bad abdominal pain, blood in your stool or if the symptoms don't ease up after three days, it's a good idea to see a doctor.

Another common ailment among travelers is sunburn. Preventing this is easy: Wear a good sunscreen that you reapply regularly, consider wearing a hat and stay out of the midday sun. If you do get sunburned, slather on the moisturizer, drink lots of water to rehydrate your skin, take some mild painkillers if you need to and avoid the sun.

Avoid getting bitten or stung by insects such as mosquitoes, ticks and sandflies. Not only are these bites irritatingly itchy and sometimes downright painful but the insects may also transmit serious diseases, including malaria. To prevent insect bites and stings, a good insect repellent will normally do the trick.

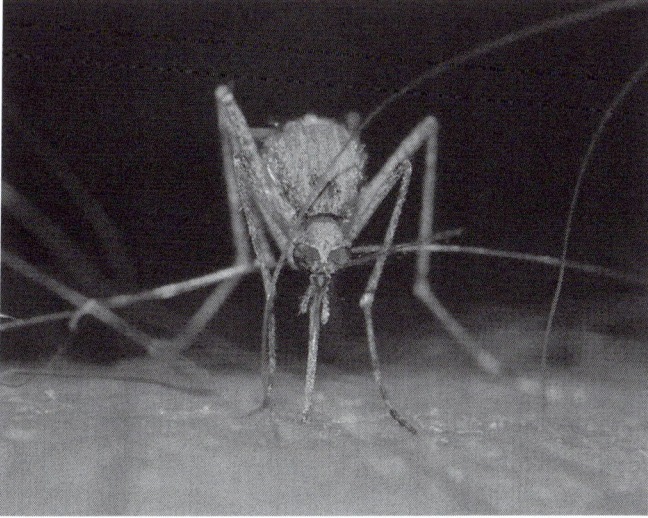

By all means, read up about more serious health risks at your destination but don't let the information scare you or turn you into a hypochondriac. A bit of a headache does not automatically mean you have dengue fever.

If you're going to go on a wilderness hike, you may want to carry a first-aid kit with you and know some basic first aid. This can save your life if you're miles away from help.

Staying safe

The golden rule for staying safe and reducing the risk of become a crime victim during your travels is to ask yourself what you would do if you were at home. Would you walk alone through a deserted park late at night? Probably not. So why would it be any safer to do that in a foreign city? Here are some other basic safety tips:

- Don't leave your belongings unattended. Not even for a few seconds. Thieves are much quicker than you'd imagine.

- Be alert. Part of being alert is not to become so drunk or stoned that you don't know where you are. Travelers who are 'out of it' are much more vulnerable to criminals.

- Be aware of common scams.

- Blend in so that you don't look like an obvious tourist. This means checking your guide book before you go out so you won't have to do it on a street corner. It also means dressing more or less like the locals do.

- Don't advertise your valuables. For instance, keep your camera in your day pack, out of sight, and only take it out when you want to take a picture. Also leave the expensive jewelry at home.

- Hide your money and bank cards in different places, for instance a bit in your backpack, a bit in your day pack and a bit in a hidden pocket or money belt. Don't even think about wearing a fanny pack that everyone can see.

- Don't pack your valuables in easily-accessed outer pockets of your backpack or day pack.

- Don't assume that you won't need to be careful in your hostel too. Unfortunately, not all your fellow travelers are honest and moral people.

- A Pacsafe, which is basically a wire mesh covering for your backpack, may give you some peace of mind. Remember though that these are quite heavy and expensive.

- Never go into the wilderness or for a hike on your own. Always do so with someone you can trust. When you hire a guide, be sure that he or she is an official guide recommended by your hostel or travel agent.

- Listen to the locals. If they tell you not to go into a certain area, don't.

- Don't get involved in any illegal dealings, such as drug deals or prostitution, since these will let you get far too close to shady characters.

Once again, it's essential to research your destination before you go. You don't want to arrive in a country only to find out that there is a civil war raging. Check your country's travel advisory to see what the security situation is and whether there is a risk of terrorism or kidnapping, for example. (If your country doesn't have this service, the US Bureau of Consular Affairs is a good alternative.) Some of these travel advisories can make things sound worse than they actually are, so don't let them put you off your plans entirely. However, they will help you get an idea of what the risks are and what precautions to take.

Useful links

For information about required and recommended vaccinations, health risks and health advice by country: http://www.who.int/ith/en/, http://www.netdoctor.co.uk/travel/vaccines_index.shtml or http://www.mdtravelhealth.com/

US travel advisory: http://travel.state.gov/content/passports/english/alertswarnings.html

Canada travel advisory: http://travel.gc.ca/travelling/advisories

UK travel advisory: https://www.gov.uk/foreign-travel-advice

Australia travel advisory: http://www.smartraveller.gov.au/

For more on common travel scams: http://wikitravel.org/en/Common_scams, http://www.lonelyplanet.com/travel-tips-and-articles/75907 or http://www.telegraph.co.uk/travel/travelnews/10980488/40-tourist-scams-to-avoid.html

Conclusion

Thank you again for downloading this book!

I hope this book was able to help you to figure out where to start when planning your backpacking trip.

The next step is to unleash your adventurous spirit, get on that airplane and go enjoy yourself! Remember to keep an open mind and not to sweat the small stuff.

Thank you, good luck and safe travels!

14044485R00035

Printed in Great Britain
by Amazon.co.uk, Ltd.,
Marston Gate.